DAILY IPA
Journal

90 Day Action Log for Income Producing Activities

Laura Aridgides, Ph.D.
www.LauraAridgides.com

ISBN: 1542468442
EAN-13: 978-1542468442

Scripture is quoted from the King James Version of the Bible.

Welcome to Daily IPA
(Income Producing Activity)

Hi there! I'm Laura. I've been a top-performing entrepreneur for nearly 18 years. I am also an author and coach, and blessed to work from home with my three children.

The heart of every successful business is focus on daily income producing activities or IPA.

When I was searching for a way to track my daily IPA, I created this form for my team and myself, and now I am sharing it with you. You have 90 days of IPA logs, and the size of this book makes it portable so you can take it with you everywhere!

The core of IPA is reaching out to new people, presenting your products, opportunity or services to those who are interested in learning more, and following up with your prospects.

Since I build my business primarily through Facebook, I added a few activities that I knew I wanted to do every day. But you can also use these suggestions in any social media platform.

I added prayer and affirmations and personal development since both are important to my personal business growth.

There is even a section to record your 90-day goals at the beginning of this book, so you will be able to look back and see how far you have come.

I challenge you to make a goal, commit to consistent daily IPA and watch your business soar!

To your success,

Laura ☺

www.LauraAridgides.com

Abbreviations Key for Notes

- ❖ **BR** – Message sent to build the relationship or reconnect.
- ❖ **CALL** – Phone call with prospect.
- ❖ **CM** – General message sent to a cold market contact.
- ❖ **CME** – General message sent to a cold market fellow entrepreneur.
- ❖ **CS** – Call scheduled.
- ❖ **CUST** – Potential customer.
- ❖ **FUB** – Followed up about business.
- ❖ **FUP** – Followed up about products.
- ❖ **HMP** – Message sent to a hot market prospect about the business or products.
- ❖ **I** – Invited to event (webinar, home meeting, etc.)
- ❖ **NIBR** – Message sent to someone who is not interested, asking for a business referral.
- ❖ **NICR** – Message sent to someone who is not interested, asking for a customer referral.
- ❖ **S** – Sent message about a special offer.
- ❖ **SAMP** – Sent prospect a product sample.
- ❖ **TPT** – Sent prospect a third-party tool (video, brochure, webinar, etc.)
- ❖ **VID** – Followed up after prospect watched a video or webinar.
- ❖ _____
- ❖ _____
- ❖ _____
- ❖ _____
- ❖ _____

My 90 Day Goals

My WHY: _____
_____
_____
_____
_____
_____
_____
_____

Where I Am Now: _____(month)
    Current Rank: _____
    Last Month's Personal Volume: _____
    Last Month's Personal Sponsoring: _____
    Last Month's Team Volume: _____
    Last Month's Team Sponsoring: _____

My Goals For Next Month: _____(month)
    Rank: _____
    Personal Volume: _____
    Personal Sponsoring: _____
    Team Volume: _____
    Team Sponsoring: _____

Where I Want to Be in 90 Days: _____(month)
    Rank: _____
    Personal Volume: _____
    Personal Sponsoring: _____
    Team Volume: _____
    Team Sponsoring: _____

Date: _____

◯ Prayer and Affirmations

Facebook
◯ Personal Post
◯ Business Post
◯ Birthdays
◯ Add 3 New Friends
    ◯ _____
    ◯ _____
    ◯ _____

Message 5-10 New People Build Relationships & Invite to Learn More
◯ _____
◯ _____
◯ _____
◯ _____
◯ _____
◯ _____
◯ _____
◯ _____
◯ _____
◯ _____

Present Business or Products to 1-3 People
◯ _____
◯ _____
◯ _____

Follow Up With 5-10 People Potentials, Customers, and Team Members

O _____
O _____
O _____
O _____
O _____
O _____
O _____
O _____
O _____
O _____

HOT Prospects and Notes:

_____
_____
_____
_____
_____
_____
_____
_____
_____
_____
_____

Personal Development
O Training Video _____
O Reading _____

I can do all things through Christ which strengtheneth me.
Phillipians 4:13

Date: _____

O Prayer and Affirmations

Facebook
O Personal Post
O Business Post
O Birthdays
O Add 3 New Friends
    O _____
    O _____
    O _____

Message 5-10 New People   Build Relationships & Invite to Learn More
O _____
O _____
O _____
O _____
O _____
O _____
O _____
O _____
O _____
O _____

Present Business or Products to 1-3 People
O _____
O _____
O _____

Follow Up With 5-10 People Potentials, Customers, and Team Members

○ _____
○ _____
○ _____
○ _____
○ _____
○ _____
○ _____
○ _____
○ _____
○ _____

HOT Prospects and Notes:

_____
_____
_____
_____
_____
_____
_____
_____
_____
_____
_____

Personal Development
○ Training Video _____
○ Reading _____

I can do all things through Christ which strengtheneth me.
Phillipians 4:13

Date: _____

○ Prayer and Affirmations

Facebook
○ Personal Post
○ Business Post
○ Birthdays
○ Add 3 New Friends
    ○ _____
    ○ _____
    ○ _____

Message 5-10 New People Build Relationships & Invite to Learn More
○ _____
○ _____
○ _____
○ _____
○ _____
○ _____
○ _____
○ _____
○ _____
○ _____

Present Business or Products to 1-3 People
○ _____
○ _____
○ _____

Follow Up With 5-10 People Potentials, Customers, and Team Members

O _____
O _____
O _____
O _____
O _____
O _____
O _____
O _____
O _____
O _____

HOT Prospects and Notes:

_____

_____

_____

_____

_____

_____

_____

_____

_____

_____

Personal Development
O Training Video _____
O Reading _____

I can do all things through Christ which strengtheneth me.
Phillipians 4:13

Date: _____

O Prayer and Affirmations

Facebook
O Personal Post
O Business Post
O Birthdays
O Add 3 New Friends
     O _____
     O _____
     O _____

Message 5-10 New People Build Relationships & Invite to Learn More
O _____
O _____
O _____
O _____
O _____
O _____
O _____
O _____
O _____
O _____

Present Business or Products to 1-3 People
O _____
O _____
O _____

Follow Up With 5-10 People Potentials, Customers, and Team Members

O _____
O _____
O _____
O _____
O _____
O _____
O _____
O _____
O _____
O _____

HOT Prospects and Notes:

_____
_____
_____
_____
_____
_____
_____
_____
_____
_____
_____

Personal Development
O Training Video _____
O Reading _____

I can do all things through Christ which strengtheneth me.
Phillipians 4:13

Date: _____

O Prayer and Affirmations

Facebook
O Personal Post
O Business Post
O Birthdays
O Add 3 New Friends
    O _____
    O _____
    O _____

Message 5-10 New People Build Relationships & Invite to Learn More
O _____
O _____
O _____
O _____
O _____
O _____
O _____
O _____
O _____
O _____

Present Business or Products to 1-3 People
O _____
O _____
O _____

Follow Up With 5-10 People Potentials, Customers, and Team Members

- ○ _____
- ○ _____
- ○ _____
- ○ _____
- ○ _____
- ○ _____
- ○ _____
- ○ _____
- ○ _____
- ○ _____

HOT Prospects and Notes:

_____

_____

_____

_____

_____

_____

_____

_____

_____

_____

_____

Personal Development
- ○ Training Video _____
- ○ Reading _____

I can do all things through Christ which strengtheneth me.
Phillipians 4:13

Date: _____

O Prayer and Affirmations

Facebook
O Personal Post
O Business Post
O Birthdays
O Add 3 New Friends
    O _____
    O _____
    O _____

Message 5-10 New People Build Relationships & Invite to Learn More
O _____
O _____
O _____
O _____
O _____
O _____
O _____
O _____
O _____
O _____

Present Business or Products to 1-3 People
O _____
O _____
O _____

Follow Up With 5-10 People Potentials, Customers, and Team Members

O _____
O _____
O _____
O _____
O _____
O _____
O _____
O _____
O _____
O _____

HOT Prospects and Notes:

_____
_____
_____
_____
_____
_____
_____
_____
_____
_____
_____

Personal Development
O Training Video _____
O Reading _____

*I can do all things through Christ which strengtheneth me.
Phillipians 4:13*

Date: _____

O Prayer and Affirmations

Facebook
O Personal Post
O Business Post
O Birthdays
O Add 3 New Friends
     O _____
     O _____
     O _____

Message 5-10 New People Build Relationships & Invite to Learn More
O _____
O _____
O _____
O _____
O _____
O _____
O _____
O _____
O _____
O _____

Present Business or Products to 1-3 People
O _____
O _____
O _____

Follow Up With 5-10 People Potentials, Customers, and Team Members

○ _____
○ _____
○ _____
○ _____
○ _____
○ _____
○ _____
○ _____
○ _____
○ _____

HOT Prospects and Notes:

_____
_____
_____
_____
_____
_____
_____
_____
_____
_____

Personal Development
○ Training Video _____
○ Reading _____

I can do all things through Christ which strengtheneth me.
Phillipians 4:13

Date: _____

O Prayer and Affirmations

Facebook
O Personal Post
O Business Post
O Birthdays
O Add 3 New Friends
    O _____
    O _____
    O _____

Message 5-10 New People Build Relationships & Invite to Learn More
O _____
O _____
O _____
O _____
O _____
O _____
O _____
O _____
O _____
O _____

Present Business or Products to 1-3 People
O _____
O _____
O _____

Follow Up With 5-10 People Potentials, Customers, and Team Members

O _____
O _____
O _____
O _____
O _____
O _____
O _____
O _____
O _____
O _____

HOT Prospects and Notes:

_____

_____

_____

_____

_____

_____

_____

_____

_____

_____

_____

Personal Development
O Training Video _____
O Reading _____

I can do all things through Christ which strengtheneth me.
Phillipians 4:13

Date: _____

O Prayer and Affirmations

Facebook
O Personal Post
O Business Post
O Birthdays
O Add 3 New Friends
    O _____
    O _____
    O _____

Message 5-10 New People Build Relationships & Invite to Learn More
O _____
O _____
O _____
O _____
O _____
O _____
O _____
O _____
O _____
O _____

Present Business or Products to 1-3 People
O _____
O _____
O _____

Follow Up With 5-10 People Potentials, Customers, and Team Members

O _____
O _____
O _____
O _____
O _____
O _____
O _____
O _____
O _____
O _____

HOT Prospects and Notes:

_____
_____
_____
_____
_____
_____
_____
_____
_____
_____
_____

Personal Development
O Training Video _____
O Reading _____

I can do all things through Christ which strengtheneth me.
Phillipians 4:13

Date: _____

O Prayer and Affirmations

Facebook
O Personal Post
O Business Post
O Birthdays
O Add 3 New Friends
    O _____
    O _____
    O _____

Message 5-10 New People Build Relationships & Invite to Learn More
O _____
O _____
O _____
O _____
O _____
O _____
O _____
O _____
O _____
O _____

Present Business or Products to 1-3 People
O _____
O _____
O _____

Follow Up With 5-10 People Potentials, Customers, and Team Members

○ _____
○ _____
○ _____
○ _____
○ _____
○ _____
○ _____
○ _____
○ _____
○ _____

HOT Prospects and Notes:

_____
_____
_____
_____
_____
_____
_____
_____
_____
_____
_____

Personal Development
○ Training Video _____
○ Reading _____

I can do all things through Christ which strengtheneth me.
Phillipians 4:13

Date: _____

O Prayer and Affirmations

Facebook
O Personal Post
O Business Post
O Birthdays
O Add 3 New Friends
     O _____
     O _____
     O _____

Message 5-10 New People Build Relationships & Invite to Learn More
O _____
O _____
O _____
O _____
O _____
O _____
O _____
O _____
O _____
O _____

Present Business or Products to 1-3 People
O _____
O _____
O _____

Follow Up With 5-10 People Potentials, Customers, and Team Members

○ _____
○ _____
○ _____
○ _____
○ _____
○ _____
○ _____
○ _____
○ _____
○ _____

HOT Prospects and Notes:

_____
_____
_____
_____
_____
_____
_____
_____
_____
_____

Personal Development
○ Training Video _____
○ Reading _____

I can do all things through Christ which strengtheneth me.
Phillipians 4:13

Date: _____

O Prayer and Affirmations

Facebook
O Personal Post
O Business Post
O Birthdays
O Add 3 New Friends
    O _____
    O _____
    O _____

Message 5-10 New People Build Relationships & Invite to Learn More
O _____
O _____
O _____
O _____
O _____
O _____
O _____
O _____
O _____
O _____

Present Business or Products to 1-3 People
O _____
O _____
O _____

Follow Up With 5-10 People Potentials, Customers, and Team Members

○ _____
○ _____
○ _____
○ _____
○ _____
○ _____
○ _____
○ _____
○ _____
○ _____

HOT Prospects and Notes:

_____
_____
_____
_____
_____
_____
_____
_____
_____
_____
_____

Personal Development
○ Training Video _____
○ Reading _____

I can do all things through Christ which strengtheneth me.
Phillipians 4:13

Date: _____

O Prayer and Affirmations

Facebook
O Personal Post
O Business Post
O Birthdays
O Add 3 New Friends
    O _____
    O _____
    O _____

Message 5-10 New People Build Relationships & Invite to Learn More
O _____
O _____
O _____
O _____
O _____
O _____
O _____
O _____
O _____
O _____

Present Business or Products to 1-3 People
O _____
O _____
O _____

Follow Up With 5-10 People Potentials, Customers, and Team Members

O _____

O _____

O _____

O _____

O _____

O _____

O _____

O _____

O _____

O _____

HOT Prospects and Notes:

_____

_____

_____

_____

_____

_____

_____

_____

_____

_____

Personal Development

O Training Video _____

O Reading _____

I can do all things through Christ which strengtheneth me.
Phillipians 4:13

Date: _____

O Prayer and Affirmations

Facebook
O Personal Post
O Business Post
O Birthdays
O Add 3 New Friends
     O _____
     O _____
     O _____

Message 5-10 New People Build Relationships & Invite to Learn More
O _____
O _____
O _____
O _____
O _____
O _____
O _____
O _____
O _____
O _____

Present Business or Products to 1-3 People
O _____
O _____
O _____

Follow Up With 5-10 People Potentials, Customers, and Team Members

○ _____
○ _____
○ _____
○ _____
○ _____
○ _____
○ _____
○ _____
○ _____
○ _____

HOT Prospects and Notes:

_____
_____
_____
_____
_____
_____
_____
_____
_____
_____
_____

Personal Development
○ Training Video _____
○ Reading _____

I can do all things through Christ which strengtheneth me.
Phillipians 4:13

Date: _____

O Prayer and Affirmations

Facebook
O Personal Post
O Business Post
O Birthdays
O Add 3 New Friends
    O _____
    O _____
    O _____

Message 5-10 New People Build Relationships & Invite to Learn More
O _____
O _____
O _____
O _____
O _____
O _____
O _____
O _____
O _____
O _____

Present Business or Products to 1-3 People
O _____
O _____
O _____

Follow Up With 5-10 People Potentials, Customers, and Team Members

○ _____
○ _____
○ _____
○ _____
○ _____
○ _____
○ _____
○ _____
○ _____
○ _____

HOT Prospects and Notes:

_____
_____
_____
_____
_____
_____
_____
_____
_____
_____
_____

Personal Development
○ Training Video _____
○ Reading _____

I can do all things through Christ which strengtheneth me.
Phillipians 4:13

Date: _____

O Prayer and Affirmations

Facebook
O Personal Post
O Business Post
O Birthdays
O Add 3 New Friends
    O _____
    O _____
    O _____

Message 5-10 New People Build Relationships & Invite to Learn More
O _____
O _____
O _____
O _____
O _____
O _____
O _____
O _____
O _____
O _____

Present Business or Products to 1-3 People
O _____
O _____
O _____

Follow Up With 5-10 People Potentials, Customers, and Team Members

O _____
O _____
O _____
O _____
O _____
O _____
O _____
O _____
O _____
O _____

HOT Prospects and Notes:

_____
_____
_____
_____
_____
_____
_____
_____
_____
_____

Personal Development
O Training Video _____
O Reading _____

I can do all things through Christ which strengtheneth me.
Phillipians 4:13

Date: _____

○ Prayer and Affirmations

Facebook
○ Personal Post
○ Business Post
○ Birthdays
○ Add 3 New Friends
    ○ _____
    ○ _____
    ○ _____

Message 5-10 New People Build Relationships & Invite to Learn More
○ _____
○ _____
○ _____
○ _____
○ _____
○ _____
○ _____
○ _____
○ _____
○ _____

Present Business or Products to 1-3 People
○ _____
○ _____
○ _____

Follow Up With 5-10 People <small>Potentials, Customers, and Team Members</small>

○ _____
○ _____
○ _____
○ _____
○ _____
○ _____
○ _____
○ _____
○ _____
○ _____

HOT Prospects and Notes:

_____
_____
_____
_____
_____
_____
_____
_____
_____
_____

Personal Development
○ Training Video _____
○ Reading _____

I can do all things through Christ which strengtheneth me.
Phillipians 4:13

Date: _____

O Prayer and Affirmations

Facebook
O Personal Post
O Business Post
O Birthdays
O Add 3 New Friends
    O _____
    O _____
    O _____

Message 5-10 New People Build Relationships & Invite to Learn More
O _____
O _____
O _____
O _____
O _____
O _____
O _____
O _____
O _____
O _____

Present Business or Products to 1-3 People
O _____
O _____
O _____

Follow Up With 5-10 People Potentials, Customers, and Team Members

O _____

O _____

O _____

O _____

O _____

O _____

O _____

O _____

O _____

O _____

HOT Prospects and Notes:

_____

_____

_____

_____

_____

_____

_____

_____

_____

_____

Personal Development
O Training Video _____

O Reading _____

I can do all things through Christ which strengtheneth me.
Phillipians 4:13

Date: _____

O Prayer and Affirmations

Facebook
O Personal Post
O Business Post
O Birthdays
O Add 3 New Friends
　　　O _____
　　　O _____
　　　O _____

Message 5-10 New People Build Relationships & Invite to Learn More
O _____
O _____
O _____
O _____
O _____
O _____
O _____
O _____
O _____
O _____

Present Business or Products to 1-3 People
O _____
O _____
O _____

Follow Up With 5-10 People Potentials, Customers, and Team Members

○ _____
○ _____
○ _____
○ _____
○ _____
○ _____
○ _____
○ _____
○ _____
○ _____

HOT Prospects and Notes:

_____
_____
_____
_____
_____
_____
_____
_____
_____
_____

Personal Development
○ Training Video _____
○ Reading _____

I can do all things through Christ which strengtheneth me.
Phillipians 4:13

Date: _____

O Prayer and Affirmations

Facebook
O Personal Post
O Business Post
O Birthdays
O Add 3 New Friends
    O _____
    O _____
    O _____

Message 5-10 New People Build Relationships & Invite to Learn More
O _____
O _____
O _____
O _____
O _____
O _____
O _____
O _____
O _____
O _____

Present Business or Products to 1-3 People
O _____
O _____
O _____

Follow Up With 5-10 People Potentials, Customers, and Team Members

○ _____
○ _____
○ _____
○ _____
○ _____
○ _____
○ _____
○ _____
○ _____
○ _____

HOT Prospects and Notes:

_____
_____
_____
_____
_____
_____
_____
_____
_____
_____

Personal Development
○ Training Video _____
○ Reading _____

I can do all things through Christ which strengtheneth me.
Phillipians 4:13

Date: _____

O Prayer and Affirmations

Facebook
O Personal Post
O Business Post
O Birthdays
O Add 3 New Friends
    O _____
    O _____
    O _____

Message 5-10 New People Build Relationships & Invite to Learn More
O _____
O _____
O _____
O _____
O _____
O _____
O _____
O _____
O _____
O _____

Present Business or Products to 1-3 People
O _____
O _____
O _____

Follow Up With 5-10 People <small>Potentials, Customers, and Team Members</small>

○ _____
○ _____
○ _____
○ _____
○ _____
○ _____
○ _____
○ _____
○ _____
○ _____

HOT Prospects and Notes:

_____
_____
_____
_____
_____
_____
_____
_____
_____

Personal Development
○ Training Video _____
○ Reading _____

I can do all things through Christ which strengtheneth me.
Phillipians 4:13

Date: _____

O Prayer and Affirmations

Facebook
O Personal Post
O Business Post
O Birthdays
O Add 3 New Friends
    O _____
    O _____
    O _____

Message 5-10 New People Build Relationships & Invite to Learn More
O _____
O _____
O _____
O _____
O _____
O _____
O _____
O _____
O _____
O _____

Present Business or Products to 1-3 People
O _____
O _____
O _____

Follow Up With 5-10 People Potentials, Customers, and Team Members

○ _____
○ _____
○ _____
○ _____
○ _____
○ _____
○ _____
○ _____
○ _____
○ _____

HOT Prospects and Notes:

_____
_____
_____
_____
_____
_____
_____
_____
_____
_____
_____

Personal Development
○ Training Video _____
○ Reading _____

I can do all things through Christ which strengtheneth me.
Phillipians 4:13

Date: _____

O Prayer and Affirmations

Facebook
O Personal Post
O Business Post
O Birthdays
O Add 3 New Friends
    O _____
    O _____
    O _____

Message 5-10 New People Build Relationships & Invite to Learn More
O _____
O _____
O _____
O _____
O _____
O _____
O _____
O _____
O _____
O _____

Present Business or Products to 1-3 People
O _____
O _____
O _____

Follow Up With 5-10 People Potentials, Customers, and Team Members

○ _____
○ _____
○ _____
○ _____
○ _____
○ _____
○ _____
○ _____
○ _____
○ _____

HOT Prospects and Notes:

_____
_____
_____
_____
_____
_____
_____
_____
_____
_____

Personal Development
○ Training Video _____
○ Reading _____

I can do all things through Christ which strengtheneth me.
Phillipians 4:13

Date: _____

O Prayer and Affirmations

Facebook
O Personal Post
O Business Post
O Birthdays
O Add 3 New Friends
    O _____
    O _____
    O _____

Message 5-10 New People Build Relationships & Invite to Learn More
O _____
O _____
O _____
O _____
O _____
O _____
O _____
O _____
O _____
O _____

Present Business or Products to 1-3 People
O _____
O _____
O _____

Follow Up With 5-10 People Potentials, Customers, and Team Members

O _____
O _____
O _____
O _____
O _____
O _____
O _____
O _____
O _____
O _____

HOT Prospects and Notes:

_____
_____
_____
_____
_____
_____
_____
_____
_____
_____

Personal Development
O Training Video _____
O Reading _____

I can do all things through Christ which strengtheneth me.
Phillipians 4:13

Date: _____

O Prayer and Affirmations

Facebook
O Personal Post
O Business Post
O Birthdays
O Add 3 New Friends
    O _____
    O _____
    O _____

Message 5-10 New People Build Relationships & Invite to Learn More
O _____
O _____
O _____
O _____
O _____
O _____
O _____
O _____
O _____
O _____

Present Business or Products to 1-3 People
O _____
O _____
O _____

Follow Up With 5-10 People Potentials, Customers, and Team Members

O _____

O _____

O _____

O _____

O _____

O _____

O _____

O _____

O _____

O _____

HOT Prospects and Notes:

_____

_____

_____

_____

_____

_____

_____

_____

_____

_____

Personal Development
O Training Video _____
O Reading _____

I can do all things through Christ which strengtheneth me.
Phillipians 4:13

Date: _____

O Prayer and Affirmations

Facebook
O Personal Post
O Business Post
O Birthdays
O Add 3 New Friends
    O _____
    O _____
    O _____

Message 5-10 New People Build Relationships & Invite to Learn More
O _____
O _____
O _____
O _____
O _____
O _____
O _____
O _____
O _____
O _____

Present Business or Products to 1-3 People
O _____
O _____
O _____

Follow Up With 5-10 People Potentials, Customers, and Team Members

O _____
O _____
O _____
O _____
O _____
O _____
O _____
O _____
O _____
O _____

HOT Prospects and Notes:

_____
_____
_____
_____
_____
_____
_____
_____
_____
_____
_____

Personal Development
O Training Video _____
O Reading _____

I can do all things through Christ which strengtheneth me.
Phillipians 4:13

Date: _____

○ Prayer and Affirmations

Facebook
○ Personal Post
○ Business Post
○ Birthdays
○ Add 3 New Friends
    ○ _____
    ○ _____
    ○ _____

Message 5-10 New People Build Relationships & Invite to Learn More
○ _____
○ _____
○ _____
○ _____
○ _____
○ _____
○ _____
○ _____
○ _____
○ _____

Present Business or Products to 1-3 People
○ _____
○ _____
○ _____

Follow Up With 5-10 People Potentials, Customers, and Team Members

○ _____
○ _____
○ _____
○ _____
○ _____
○ _____
○ _____
○ _____
○ _____
○ _____

HOT Prospects and Notes:

_____
_____
_____
_____
_____
_____
_____
_____
_____
_____
_____

Personal Development
○ Training Video _____
○ Reading _____

I can do all things through Christ which strengtheneth me.
Phillipians 4:13

Date: _____

O Prayer and Affirmations

Facebook
O Personal Post
O Business Post
O Birthdays
O Add 3 New Friends
     O _____
     O _____
     O _____

Message 5-10 New People Build Relationships & Invite to Learn More
O _____
O _____
O _____
O _____
O _____
O _____
O _____
O _____
O _____
O _____

Present Business or Products to 1-3 People
O _____
O _____
O _____

Follow Up With 5-10 People Potentials, Customers, and Team Members

○ _____
○ _____
○ _____
○ _____
○ _____
○ _____
○ _____
○ _____
○ _____
○ _____

HOT Prospects and Notes:

_____
_____
_____
_____
_____
_____
_____
_____
_____
_____
_____

Personal Development
○ Training Video _____
○ Reading _____

I can do all things through Christ which strengtheneth me.
Phillipians 4:13

Date: _____

O Prayer and Affirmations

Facebook
O Personal Post
O Business Post
O Birthdays
O Add 3 New Friends
    O _____
    O _____
    O _____

Message 5-10 New People Build Relationships & Invite to Learn More
O _____
O _____
O _____
O _____
O _____
O _____
O _____
O _____
O _____
O _____

Present Business or Products to 1-3 People
O _____
O _____
O _____

Follow Up With 5-10 People Potentials, Customers, and Team Members

○ _____
○ _____
○ _____
○ _____
○ _____
○ _____
○ _____
○ _____
○ _____
○ _____

HOT Prospects and Notes:

_____
_____
_____
_____
_____
_____
_____
_____
_____
_____
_____

Personal Development
○ Training Video _____
○ Reading _____

I can do all things through Christ which strengtheneth me.
Phillipians 4:13

Date: _____

O Prayer and Affirmations

Facebook
O Personal Post
O Business Post
O Birthdays
O Add 3 New Friends
    O _____
    O _____
    O _____

Message 5-10 New People Build Relationships & Invite to Learn More
O _____
O _____
O _____
O _____
O _____
O _____
O _____
O _____
O _____
O _____

Present Business or Products to 1-3 People
O _____
O _____
O _____

Follow Up With 5-10 People Potentials, Customers, and Team Members

O _____
O _____
O _____
O _____
O _____
O _____
O _____
O _____
O _____
O _____

HOT Prospects and Notes:

_____
_____
_____
_____
_____
_____
_____
_____
_____
_____
_____

Personal Development
O Training Video _____
O Reading _____

I can do all things through Christ which strengtheneth me.
Phillipians 4:13

Date: _____

O Prayer and Affirmations

Facebook
O Personal Post
O Business Post
O Birthdays
O Add 3 New Friends
    O _____
    O _____
    O _____

Message 5-10 New People Build Relationships & Invite to Learn More
O _____
O _____
O _____
O _____
O _____
O _____
O _____
O _____
O _____
O _____

Present Business or Products to 1-3 People
O _____
O _____
O _____

Follow Up With 5-10 People Potentials, Customers, and Team Members

○ _____
○ _____
○ _____
○ _____
○ _____
○ _____
○ _____
○ _____
○ _____
○ _____

HOT Prospects and Notes:

_____
_____
_____
_____
_____
_____
_____
_____
_____
_____

Personal Development
○ Training Video _____
○ Reading _____

I can do all things through Christ which strengtheneth me.
Phillipians 4:13

Date: _____

O Prayer and Affirmations

Facebook
O Personal Post
O Business Post
O Birthdays
O Add 3 New Friends
    O _____
    O _____
    O _____

Message 5-10 New People Build Relationships & Invite to Learn More
O _____
O _____
O _____
O _____
O _____
O _____
O _____
O _____
O _____
O _____

Present Business or Products to 1-3 People
O _____
O _____
O _____

Follow Up With 5-10 People Potentials, Customers, and Team Members

O _____
O _____
O _____
O _____
O _____
O _____
O _____
O _____
O _____
O _____

HOT Prospects and Notes:

_____
_____
_____
_____
_____
_____
_____
_____
_____
_____
_____

Personal Development
O Training Video _____
O Reading _____

I can do all things through Christ which strengtheneth me.
Phillipians 4:13

Date: _____

O Prayer and Affirmations

Facebook
O Personal Post
O Business Post
O Birthdays
O Add 3 New Friends
    O _____
    O _____
    O _____

Message 5-10 New People Build Relationships & Invite to Learn More
O _____
O _____
O _____
O _____
O _____
O _____
O _____
O _____
O _____
O _____

Present Business or Products to 1-3 People
O _____
O _____
O _____

Follow Up With 5-10 People Potentials, Customers, and Team Members

O _____
O _____
O _____
O _____
O _____
O _____
O _____
O _____
O _____
O _____

HOT Prospects and Notes:

_____
_____
_____
_____
_____
_____
_____
_____
_____
_____

Personal Development
O Training Video _____
O Reading _____

I can do all things through Christ which strengtheneth me.
Phillipians 4:13

Date: _____

O Prayer and Affirmations

Facebook
O Personal Post
O Business Post
O Birthdays
O Add 3 New Friends
    O _____
    O _____
    O _____

Message 5-10 New People Build Relationships & Invite to Learn More
O _____
O _____
O _____
O _____
O _____
O _____
O _____
O _____
O _____
O _____

Present Business or Products to 1-3 People
O _____
O _____
O _____

Follow Up With 5-10 People Potentials, Customers, and Team Members

O _____
O _____
O _____
O _____
O _____
O _____
O _____
O _____
O _____
O _____

HOT Prospects and Notes:

_____
_____
_____
_____
_____
_____
_____
_____
_____
_____

Personal Development
O Training Video _____
O Reading _____

I can do all things through Christ which strengtheneth me.
Phillipians 4:13

Date: _____

O Prayer and Affirmations

Facebook
O Personal Post
O Business Post
O Birthdays
O Add 3 New Friends
    O _____
    O _____
    O _____

Message 5-10 New People Build Relationships & Invite to Learn More
O _____
O _____
O _____
O _____
O _____
O _____
O _____
O _____
O _____
O _____

Present Business or Products to 1-3 People
O _____
O _____
O _____

Follow Up With 5-10 People <small>Potentials, Customers, and Team Members</small>

O _____
O _____
O _____
O _____
O _____
O _____
O _____
O _____
O _____
O _____

HOT Prospects and Notes:

_____
_____
_____
_____
_____
_____
_____
_____
_____
_____

Personal Development
O Training Video _____
O Reading _____

I can do all things through Christ which strengtheneth me.
Phillipians 4:13

Date: _____

○ Prayer and Affirmations

Facebook
○ Personal Post
○ Business Post
○ Birthdays
○ Add 3 New Friends
     ○ _____
     ○ _____
     ○ _____

Message 5-10 New People Build Relationships & Invite to Learn More
○ _____
○ _____
○ _____
○ _____
○ _____
○ _____
○ _____
○ _____
○ _____
○ _____

Present Business or Products to 1-3 People
○ _____
○ _____
○ _____

Follow Up With 5-10 People <small>Potentials, Customers, and Team Members</small>

O _____
O _____
O _____
O _____
O _____
O _____
O _____
O _____
O _____
O _____

HOT Prospects and Notes:

_____
_____
_____
_____
_____
_____
_____
_____
_____
_____
_____

Personal Development
O Training Video _____
O Reading _____

I can do all things through Christ which strengtheneth me.
Phillipians 4:13

Date: _____

O Prayer and Affirmations

Facebook
O Personal Post
O Business Post
O Birthdays
O Add 3 New Friends
    O _____
    O _____
    O _____

Message 5-10 New People Build Relationships & Invite to Learn More
O _____
O _____
O _____
O _____
O _____
O _____
O _____
O _____
O _____
O _____

Present Business or Products to 1-3 People
O _____
O _____
O _____

Follow Up With 5-10 People Potentials, Customers, and Team Members

O _____
O _____
O _____
O _____
O _____
O _____
O _____
O _____
O _____
O _____

HOT Prospects and Notes:

_____
_____
_____
_____
_____
_____
_____
_____
_____
_____

Personal Development
O Training Video _____
O Reading _____

I can do all things through Christ which strengtheneth me.
Phillipians 4:13

Date: _____

O Prayer and Affirmations

Facebook
O Personal Post
O Business Post
O Birthdays
O Add 3 New Friends
    O _____
    O _____
    O _____

Message 5-10 New People Build Relationships & Invite to Learn More
O _____
O _____
O _____
O _____
O _____
O _____
O _____
O _____
O _____
O _____

Present Business or Products to 1-3 People
O _____
O _____
O _____

Follow Up With 5-10 People Potentials, Customers, and Team Members

O _____
O _____
O _____
O _____
O _____
O _____
O _____
O _____
O _____
O _____

HOT Prospects and Notes:

_____
_____
_____
_____
_____
_____
_____
_____
_____
_____

Personal Development
O Training Video _____
O Reading _____

I can do all things through Christ which strengtheneth me.
Phillipians 4:13

Date: _____

O Prayer and Affirmations

Facebook
O Personal Post
O Business Post
O Birthdays
O Add 3 New Friends
    O _____
    O _____
    O _____

Message 5-10 New People Build Relationships & Invite to Learn More
O _____
O _____
O _____
O _____
O _____
O _____
O _____
O _____
O _____
O _____

Present Business or Products to 1-3 People
O _____
O _____
O _____

Follow Up With 5-10 People Potentials, Customers, and Team Members

O _____
O _____
O _____
O _____
O _____
O _____
O _____
O _____
O _____
O _____

HOT Prospects and Notes:

_____
_____
_____
_____
_____
_____
_____
_____
_____
_____
_____

Personal Development
O Training Video _____
O Reading _____

I can do all things through Christ which strengtheneth me.
Phillipians 4:13

Date: _____

○ Prayer and Affirmations

Facebook
○ Personal Post
○ Business Post
○ Birthdays
○ Add 3 New Friends
     ○ _____
     ○ _____
     ○ _____

Message 5-10 New People Build Relationships & Invite to Learn More
○ _____
○ _____
○ _____
○ _____
○ _____
○ _____
○ _____
○ _____
○ _____
○ _____

Present Business or Products to 1-3 People
○ _____
○ _____
○ _____

Follow Up With 5-10 People Potentials, Customers, and Team Members

O _____
O _____
O _____
O _____
O _____
O _____
O _____
O _____
O _____
O _____

HOT Prospects and Notes:

_____
_____
_____
_____
_____
_____
_____
_____
_____
_____
_____

Personal Development
O Training Video _____
O Reading _____

I can do all things through Christ which strengtheneth me.
Phillipians 4:13

Date: _____

O Prayer and Affirmations

Facebook
O Personal Post
O Business Post
O Birthdays
O Add 3 New Friends
    O _____
    O _____
    O _____

Message 5-10 New People Build Relationships & Invite to Learn More
O _____
O _____
O _____
O _____
O _____
O _____
O _____
O _____
O _____
O _____

Present Business or Products to 1-3 People
O _____
O _____
O _____

Follow Up With 5-10 People Potentials, Customers, and Team Members

○ _____
○ _____
○ _____
○ _____
○ _____
○ _____
○ _____
○ _____
○ _____
○ _____

HOT Prospects and Notes:

_____
_____
_____
_____
_____
_____
_____
_____
_____
_____
_____

Personal Development
○ Training Video _____
○ Reading _____

I can do all things through Christ which strengtheneth me.
Phillipians 4:13

Date: _____

○ Prayer and Affirmations

Facebook
○ Personal Post
○ Business Post
○ Birthdays
○ Add 3 New Friends
　　　○ _____
　　　○ _____
　　　○ _____

Message 5-10 New People Build Relationships & Invite to Learn More
○ _____
○ _____
○ _____
○ _____
○ _____
○ _____
○ _____
○ _____
○ _____
○ _____

Present Business or Products to 1-3 People
○ _____
○ _____
○ _____

Follow Up With 5-10 People Potentials, Customers, and Team Members

O _____

O _____

O _____

O _____

O _____

O _____

O _____

O _____

O _____

O _____

HOT Prospects and Notes:

_____

_____

_____

_____

_____

_____

_____

_____

_____

_____

_____

Personal Development

O Training Video _____

O Reading _____

I can do all things through Christ which strengtheneth me.
Phillipians 4:13

Date: _____

O Prayer and Affirmations

Facebook
O Personal Post
O Business Post
O Birthdays
O Add 3 New Friends
    O _____
    O _____
    O _____

Message 5-10 New People Build Relationships & Invite to Learn More
O _____
O _____
O _____
O _____
O _____
O _____
O _____
O _____
O _____
O _____

Present Business or Products to 1-3 People
O _____
O _____
O _____

Follow Up With 5-10 People Potentials, Customers, and Team Members

O _____
O _____
O _____
O _____
O _____
O _____
O _____
O _____
O _____
O _____

HOT Prospects and Notes:

_____
_____
_____
_____
_____
_____
_____
_____
_____
_____

Personal Development
O Training Video _____
O Reading _____

I can do all things through Christ which strengtheneth me.
Phillipians 4:13

Date: _____

O Prayer and Affirmations

Facebook
O Personal Post
O Business Post
O Birthdays
O Add 3 New Friends
     O _____
     O _____
     O _____

Message 5-10 New People Build Relationships & Invite to Learn More
O _____
O _____
O _____
O _____
O _____
O _____
O _____
O _____
O _____
O _____

Present Business or Products to 1-3 People
O _____
O _____
O _____

Follow Up With 5-10 People Potentials, Customers, and Team Members

O _____
O _____
O _____
O _____
O _____
O _____
O _____
O _____
O _____
O _____

HOT Prospects and Notes:

_____
_____
_____
_____
_____
_____
_____
_____
_____
_____
_____
_____

Personal Development
O Training Video _____
O Reading _____

I can do all things through Christ which strengtheneth me.
Phillipians 4:13

Date: _____

O Prayer and Affirmations

Facebook
O Personal Post
O Business Post
O Birthdays
O Add 3 New Friends
    O _____
    O _____
    O _____

Message 5-10 New People <small>Build Relationships & Invite to Learn More</small>
O _____
O _____
O _____
O _____
O _____
O _____
O _____
O _____
O _____
O _____

Present Business or Products to 1-3 People
O _____
O _____
O _____

Follow Up With 5-10 People Potentials, Customers, and Team Members

O _____
O _____
O _____
O _____
O _____
O _____
O _____
O _____
O _____
O _____

HOT Prospects and Notes:

_____
_____
_____
_____
_____
_____
_____
_____
_____
_____
_____

Personal Development
O Training Video _____
O Reading _____

I can do all things through Christ which strengtheneth me.
Phillipians 4:13

Date: _____

O Prayer and Affirmations

Facebook
O Personal Post
O Business Post
O Birthdays
O Add 3 New Friends
     O _____
     O _____
     O _____

Message 5-10 New People Build Relationships & Invite to Learn More
O _____
O _____
O _____
O _____
O _____
O _____
O _____
O _____
O _____
O _____

Present Business or Products to 1-3 People
O _____
O _____
O _____

Follow Up With 5-10 People Potentials, Customers, and Team Members

O _____
O _____
O _____
O _____
O _____
O _____
O _____
O _____
O _____
O _____

HOT Prospects and Notes:

_____
_____
_____
_____
_____
_____
_____
_____
_____
_____

Personal Development
O Training Video _____
O Reading _____

I can do all things through Christ which strengtheneth me.
Phillipians 4:13

Date: _____

○ Prayer and Affirmations

Facebook
○ Personal Post
○ Business Post
○ Birthdays
○ Add 3 New Friends
    ○ _____
    ○ _____
    ○ _____

Message 5-10 New People Build Relationships & Invite to Learn More
○ _____
○ _____
○ _____
○ _____
○ _____
○ _____
○ _____
○ _____
○ _____
○ _____

Present Business or Products to 1-3 People
○ _____
○ _____
○ _____

Follow Up With 5-10 People Potentials, Customers, and Team Members

O _____
O _____
O _____
O _____
O _____
O _____
O _____
O _____
O _____
O _____

HOT Prospects and Notes:

_____
_____
_____
_____
_____
_____
_____
_____
_____
_____

Personal Development
O Training Video _____
O Reading _____

I can do all things through Christ which strengtheneth me.
Phillipians 4:13

Date: _____

O Prayer and Affirmations

Facebook
O Personal Post
O Business Post
O Birthdays
O Add 3 New Friends
     O _____
     O _____
     O _____

Message 5-10 New People Build Relationships & Invite to Learn More
O _____
O _____
O _____
O _____
O _____
O _____
O _____
O _____
O _____
O _____

Present Business or Products to 1-3 People
O _____
O _____
O _____

Follow Up With 5-10 People Potentials, Customers, and Team Members

○ _____

○ _____

○ _____

○ _____

○ _____

○ _____

○ _____

○ _____

○ _____

○ _____

HOT Prospects and Notes:

_____

_____

_____

_____

_____

_____

_____

_____

_____

_____

Personal Development
○ Training Video _____

○ Reading _____

I can do all things through Christ which strengtheneth me.
Phillipians 4:13

Date: _____

O Prayer and Affirmations

Facebook
O Personal Post
O Business Post
O Birthdays
O Add 3 New Friends
     O _____
     O _____
     O _____

Message 5-10 New People Build Relationships & Invite to Learn More
O _____
O _____
O _____
O _____
O _____
O _____
O _____
O _____
O _____
O _____

Present Business or Products to 1-3 People
O _____
O _____
O _____

Follow Up With 5-10 People Potentials, Customers, and Team Members

O _____
O _____
O _____
O _____
O _____
O _____
O _____
O _____
O _____
O _____

HOT Prospects and Notes:

_____
_____
_____
_____
_____
_____
_____
_____
_____
_____

Personal Development
O Training Video _____
O Reading _____

I can do all things through Christ which strengtheneth me.
Phillipians 4:13

Date: _____

O Prayer and Affirmations

Facebook
O Personal Post
O Business Post
O Birthdays
O Add 3 New Friends
    O _____
    O _____
    O _____

Message 5-10 New People Build Relationships & Invite to Learn More
O _____
O _____
O _____
O _____
O _____
O _____
O _____
O _____
O _____
O _____

Present Business or Products to 1-3 People
O _____
O _____
O _____

Follow Up With 5-10 People Potentials, Customers, and Team Members

O _____
O _____
O _____
O _____
O _____
O _____
O _____
O _____
O _____
O _____

HOT Prospects and Notes:

_____
_____
_____
_____
_____
_____
_____
_____
_____
_____
_____

Personal Development
O Training Video _____
O Reading _____

I can do all things through Christ which strengtheneth me.
Phillipians 4:13

Date: _____

O Prayer and Affirmations

Facebook
O Personal Post
O Business Post
O Birthdays
O Add 3 New Friends
     O _____
     O _____
     O _____

Message 5-10 New People Build Relationships & Invite to Learn More
O _____
O _____
O _____
O _____
O _____
O _____
O _____
O _____
O _____
O _____

Present Business or Products to 1-3 People
O _____
O _____
O _____

Follow Up With 5-10 People Potentials, Customers, and Team Members

O _____
O _____
O _____
O _____
O _____
O _____
O _____
O _____
O _____
O _____

HOT Prospects and Notes:

_____
_____
_____
_____
_____
_____
_____
_____
_____
_____

Personal Development
O Training Video _____
O Reading _____

I can do all things through Christ which strengtheneth me.
Phillipians 4:13

Date: _____

O Prayer and Affirmations

Facebook
O Personal Post
O Business Post
O Birthdays
O Add 3 New Friends
    O _____
    O _____
    O _____

Message 5-10 New People Build Relationships & Invite to Learn More
O _____
O _____
O _____
O _____
O _____
O _____
O _____
O _____
O _____
O _____

Present Business or Products to 1-3 People
O _____
O _____
O _____

Follow Up With 5-10 People Potentials, Customers, and Team Members

O _____
O _____
O _____
O _____
O _____
O _____
O _____
O _____
O _____
O _____

HOT Prospects and Notes:

_____
_____
_____
_____
_____
_____
_____
_____
_____
_____

Personal Development
O Training Video _____
O Reading _____

I can do all things through Christ which strengtheneth me.
Phillipians 4:13

Date: _____

O Prayer and Affirmations

Facebook
O Personal Post
O Business Post
O Birthdays
O Add 3 New Friends
    O _____
    O _____
    O _____

Message 5-10 New People Build Relationships & Invite to Learn More
O _____
O _____
O _____
O _____
O _____
O _____
O _____
O _____
O _____
O _____

Present Business or Products to 1-3 People
O _____
O _____
O _____

Follow Up With 5-10 People Potentials, Customers, and Team Members

O _____
O _____
O _____
O _____
O _____
O _____
O _____
O _____
O _____
O _____

HOT Prospects and Notes:

_____
_____
_____
_____
_____
_____
_____
_____
_____
_____

Personal Development
O Training Video _____
O Reading _____

I can do all things through Christ which strengtheneth me.
Phillipians 4:13

Date: _____

O Prayer and Affirmations

Facebook
O Personal Post
O Business Post
O Birthdays
O Add 3 New Friends
     O _____
     O _____
     O _____

Message 5-10 New People Build Relationships & Invite to Learn More
O _____
O _____
O _____
O _____
O _____
O _____
O _____
O _____
O _____
O _____

Present Business or Products to 1-3 People
O _____
O _____
O _____

Follow Up With 5-10 People Potentials, Customers, and Team Members

O _____
O _____
O _____
O _____
O _____
O _____
O _____
O _____
O _____
O _____

HOT Prospects and Notes:

_____
_____
_____
_____
_____
_____
_____
_____
_____
_____

Personal Development
O Training Video _____
O Reading _____

I can do all things through Christ which strengtheneth me.
Phillipians 4:13

Date: _____

O Prayer and Affirmations

Facebook
O Personal Post
O Business Post
O Birthdays
O Add 3 New Friends
    O _____
    O _____
    O _____

Message 5-10 New People Build Relationships & Invite to Learn More
O _____
O _____
O _____
O _____
O _____
O _____
O _____
O _____
O _____
O _____

Present Business or Products to 1-3 People
O _____
O _____
O _____

Follow Up With 5-10 People Potentials, Customers, and Team Members

O _____
O _____
O _____
O _____
O _____
O _____
O _____
O _____
O _____
O _____

HOT Prospects and Notes:

_____
_____
_____
_____
_____
_____
_____
_____
_____
_____

Personal Development
O Training Video _____
O Reading _____

I can do all things through Christ which strengtheneth me.
Phillipians 4:13

Date: _____

O Prayer and Affirmations

Facebook
O Personal Post
O Business Post
O Birthdays
O Add 3 New Friends
     O _____
     O _____
     O _____

Message 5-10 New People Build Relationships & Invite to Learn More
O _____
O _____
O _____
O _____
O _____
O _____
O _____
O _____
O _____
O _____

Present Business or Products to 1-3 People
O _____
O _____
O _____

Follow Up With 5-10 People Potentials, Customers, and Team Members

O _____
O _____
O _____
O _____
O _____
O _____
O _____
O _____
O _____
O _____

HOT Prospects and Notes:

_____
_____
_____
_____
_____
_____
_____
_____
_____
_____
_____

Personal Development
O Training Video _____
O Reading _____

I can do all things through Christ which strengtheneth me.
Phillipians 4:13

Date: _____

O Prayer and Affirmations

Facebook
O Personal Post
O Business Post
O Birthdays
O Add 3 New Friends
    O _____
    O _____
    O _____

Message 5-10 New People Build Relationships & Invite to Learn More
O _____
O _____
O _____
O _____
O _____
O _____
O _____
O _____
O _____
O _____

Present Business or Products to 1-3 People
O _____
O _____
O _____

Follow Up With 5-10 People Potentials, Customers, and Team Members

○ _____
○ _____
○ _____
○ _____
○ _____
○ _____
○ _____
○ _____
○ _____
○ _____

HOT Prospects and Notes:

_____
_____
_____
_____
_____
_____
_____
_____
_____
_____
_____

Personal Development
○ Training Video _____
○ Reading _____

I can do all things through Christ which strengtheneth me.
Phillipians 4:13

Date: _____

O Prayer and Affirmations

Facebook
O Personal Post
O Business Post
O Birthdays
O Add 3 New Friends
     O _____
     O _____
     O _____

Message 5-10 New People Build Relationships & Invite to Learn More
O _____
O _____
O _____
O _____
O _____
O _____
O _____
O _____
O _____
O _____

Present Business or Products to 1-3 People
O _____
O _____
O _____

Follow Up With 5-10 People Potentials, Customers, and Team Members

O _____
O _____
O _____
O _____
O _____
O _____
O _____
O _____
O _____
O _____

HOT Prospects and Notes:

_____
_____
_____
_____
_____
_____
_____
_____
_____
_____

Personal Development
O Training Video _____
O Reading _____

I can do all things through Christ which strengtheneth me.
Phillipians 4:13

Date: _____

O Prayer and Affirmations

Facebook
O Personal Post
O Business Post
O Birthdays
O Add 3 New Friends
    O _____
    O _____
    O _____

Message 5-10 New People Build Relationships & Invite to Learn More
O _____
O _____
O _____
O _____
O _____
O _____
O _____
O _____
O _____
O _____

Present Business or Products to 1-3 People
O _____
O _____
O _____

Follow Up With 5-10 People Potentials, Customers, and Team Members

O _____
O _____
O _____
O _____
O _____
O _____
O _____
O _____
O _____
O _____

HOT Prospects and Notes:

_____
_____
_____
_____
_____
_____
_____
_____
_____
_____
_____

Personal Development
O Training Video _____
O Reading _____

I can do all things through Christ which strengtheneth me.
Phillipians 4:13

Date: _____

O Prayer and Affirmations

Facebook
O Personal Post
O Business Post
O Birthdays
O Add 3 New Friends
    O _____
    O _____
    O _____

Message 5-10 New People Build Relationships & Invite to Learn More
O _____
O _____
O _____
O _____
O _____
O _____
O _____
O _____
O _____
O _____

Present Business or Products to 1-3 People
O _____
O _____
O _____

Follow Up With 5-10 People Potentials, Customers, and Team Members

○ _____
○ _____
○ _____
○ _____
○ _____
○ _____
○ _____
○ _____
○ _____
○ _____

HOT Prospects and Notes:

_____
_____
_____
_____
_____
_____
_____
_____
_____
_____

Personal Development
○ Training Video _____
○ Reading _____

I can do all things through Christ which strengtheneth me.
Phillipians 4:13

Date: _____

O Prayer and Affirmations

Facebook
O Personal Post
O Business Post
O Birthdays
O Add 3 New Friends
     O _____
     O _____
     O _____

Message 5-10 New People Build Relationships & Invite to Learn More
O _____
O _____
O _____
O _____
O _____
O _____
O _____
O _____
O _____
O _____

Present Business or Products to 1-3 People
O _____
O _____
O _____

Follow Up With 5-10 People _{Potentials, Customers, and Team Members}

O _____
O _____
O _____
O _____
O _____
O _____
O _____
O _____
O _____
O _____

HOT Prospects and Notes:

_____
_____
_____
_____
_____
_____
_____
_____
_____
_____

Personal Development
O Training Video _____
O Reading _____

I can do all things through Christ which strengtheneth me.
Phillipians 4:13

Date: _____

O Prayer and Affirmations

Facebook
O Personal Post
O Business Post
O Birthdays
O Add 3 New Friends
     O _____
     O _____
     O _____

Message 5-10 New People Build Relationships & Invite to Learn More
O _____
O _____
O _____
O _____
O _____
O _____
O _____
O _____
O _____
O _____

Present Business or Products to 1-3 People
O _____
O _____
O _____

Follow Up With 5-10 People Potentials, Customers, and Team Members

O _____
O _____
O _____
O _____
O _____
O _____
O _____
O _____
O _____
O _____

HOT Prospects and Notes:

_____
_____
_____
_____
_____
_____
_____
_____
_____
_____

Personal Development
O Training Video _____
O Reading _____

I can do all things through Christ which strengtheneth me.
Phillipians 4:13

Date: _____

O Prayer and Affirmations

Facebook
O Personal Post
O Business Post
O Birthdays
O Add 3 New Friends
      O _____
      O _____
      O _____

Message 5-10 New People Build Relationships & Invite to Learn More
O _____
O _____
O _____
O _____
O _____
O _____
O _____
O _____
O _____
O _____

Present Business or Products to 1-3 People
O _____
O _____
O _____

Follow Up With 5-10 People Potentials, Customers, and Team Members

○ _____
○ _____
○ _____
○ _____
○ _____
○ _____
○ _____
○ _____
○ _____
○ _____

HOT Prospects and Notes:

_____
_____
_____
_____
_____
_____
_____
_____
_____
_____
_____

Personal Development
○ Training Video _____
○ Reading _____

I can do all things through Christ which strengtheneth me.
Phillipians 4:13

Date: _____

O Prayer and Affirmations

Facebook
O Personal Post
O Business Post
O Birthdays
O Add 3 New Friends
    O _____
    O _____
    O _____

Message 5-10 New People Build Relationships & Invite to Learn More
O _____
O _____
O _____
O _____
O _____
O _____
O _____
O _____
O _____
O _____

Present Business or Products to 1-3 People
O _____
O _____
O _____

Follow Up With 5-10 People Potentials, Customers, and Team Members

O _____

O _____

O _____

O _____

O _____

O _____

O _____

O _____

O _____

O _____

HOT Prospects and Notes:

_____

_____

_____

_____

_____

_____

_____

_____

_____

_____

Personal Development
O Training Video _____
O Reading _____

I can do all things through Christ which strengtheneth me.
Phillipians 4:13

Date: _____

O Prayer and Affirmations

Facebook
O Personal Post
O Business Post
O Birthdays
O Add 3 New Friends
    O _____
    O _____
    O _____

Message 5-10 New People Build Relationships & Invite to Learn More
O _____
O _____
O _____
O _____
O _____
O _____
O _____
O _____
O _____
O _____

Present Business or Products to 1-3 People
O _____
O _____
O _____

Follow Up With 5-10 People Potentials, Customers, and Team Members

O _____
O _____
O _____
O _____
O _____
O _____
O _____
O _____
O _____
O _____

HOT Prospects and Notes:

_____
_____
_____
_____
_____
_____
_____
_____
_____
_____

Personal Development
O Training Video _____
O Reading _____

I can do all things through Christ which strengtheneth me.
Phillipians 4:13

Date: _____

O Prayer and Affirmations

Facebook
O Personal Post
O Business Post
O Birthdays
O Add 3 New Friends
     O _____
     O _____
     O _____

Message 5-10 New People Build Relationships & Invite to Learn More
O _____
O _____
O _____
O _____
O _____
O _____
O _____
O _____
O _____
O _____

Present Business or Products to 1-3 People
O _____
O _____
O _____

Follow Up With 5-10 People Potentials, Customers, and Team Members

O _____
O _____
O _____
O _____
O _____
O _____
O _____
O _____
O _____
O _____

HOT Prospects and Notes:

_____

_____

_____

_____

_____

_____

_____

_____

_____

_____

Personal Development
O Training Video _____
O Reading _____

I can do all things through Christ which strengtheneth me.
Phillipians 4:13

Date: _____

O Prayer and Affirmations

Facebook
O Personal Post
O Business Post
O Birthdays
O Add 3 New Friends
     O _____
     O _____
     O _____

Message 5-10 New People   Build Relationships & Invite to Learn More
O _____
O _____
O _____
O _____
O _____
O _____
O _____
O _____
O _____
O _____

Present Business or Products to 1-3 People
O _____
O _____
O _____

Follow Up With 5-10 People Potentials, Customers, and Team Members

O _____
O _____
O _____
O _____
O _____
O _____
O _____
O _____
O _____
O _____

HOT Prospects and Notes:

_____
_____
_____
_____
_____
_____
_____
_____
_____
_____

Personal Development
O Training Video _____
O Reading _____

I can do all things through Christ which strengtheneth me.
Phillipians 4:13

Date: _____

O Prayer and Affirmations

Facebook
O Personal Post
O Business Post
O Birthdays
O Add 3 New Friends
    O _____
    O _____
    O _____

Message 5-10 New People Build Relationships & Invite to Learn More
O _____
O _____
O _____
O _____
O _____
O _____
O _____
O _____
O _____
O _____

Present Business or Products to 1-3 People
O _____
O _____
O _____

Follow Up With 5-10 People Potentials, Customers, and Team Members

O _____
O _____
O _____
O _____
O _____
O _____
O _____
O _____
O _____
O _____

HOT Prospects and Notes:

_____
_____
_____
_____
_____
_____
_____
_____
_____
_____

Personal Development
O Training Video _____
O Reading _____

I can do all things through Christ which strengtheneth me.
Phillipians 4:13

Date: _____

O Prayer and Affirmations

Facebook
O Personal Post
O Business Post
O Birthdays
O Add 3 New Friends
    O _____
    O _____
    O _____

Message 5-10 New People Build Relationships & Invite to Learn More
O _____
O _____
O _____
O _____
O _____
O _____
O _____
O _____
O _____
O _____

Present Business or Products to 1-3 People
O _____
O _____
O _____

Follow Up With 5-10 People Potentials, Customers, and Team Members

O _____
O _____
O _____
O _____
O _____
O _____
O _____
O _____
O _____
O _____

HOT Prospects and Notes:

_____
_____
_____
_____
_____
_____
_____
_____
_____
_____

Personal Development
O Training Video _____
O Reading _____

I can do all things through Christ which strengtheneth me.
Phillipians 4:13

Date: _____

O Prayer and Affirmations

Facebook
O Personal Post
O Business Post
O Birthdays
O Add 3 New Friends
    O _____
    O _____
    O _____

Message 5-10 New People Build Relationships & Invite to Learn More
O _____
O _____
O _____
O _____
O _____
O _____
O _____
O _____
O _____
O _____

Present Business or Products to 1-3 People
O _____
O _____
O _____

Follow Up With 5-10 People Potentials, Customers, and Team Members

O _____
O _____
O _____
O _____
O _____
O _____
O _____
O _____
O _____
O _____

HOT Prospects and Notes:

_____
_____
_____
_____
_____
_____
_____
_____
_____
_____

Personal Development
O Training Video _____
O Reading _____

I can do all things through Christ which strengtheneth me.
Phillipians 4:13

Date: _____

O Prayer and Affirmations

Facebook
O Personal Post
O Business Post
O Birthdays
O Add 3 New Friends
     O _____
     O _____
     O _____

Message 5-10 New People Build Relationships & Invite to Learn More
O _____
O _____
O _____
O _____
O _____
O _____
O _____
O _____
O _____
O _____

Present Business or Products to 1-3 People
O _____
O _____
O _____

Follow Up With 5-10 People <small>Potentials, Customers, and Team Members</small>

O _____

O _____

O _____

O _____

O _____

O _____

O _____

O _____

O _____

O _____

HOT Prospects and Notes:

_____

_____

_____

_____

_____

_____

_____

_____

_____

_____

Personal Development
O Training Video _____

O Reading _____

I can do all things through Christ which strengtheneth me.
Phillipians 4:13

Date: _____

O Prayer and Affirmations

Facebook
O Personal Post
O Business Post
O Birthdays
O Add 3 New Friends
    O _____
    O _____
    O _____

Message 5-10 New People Build Relationships & Invite to Learn More
O _____
O _____
O _____
O _____
O _____
O _____
O _____
O _____
O _____
O _____

Present Business or Products to 1-3 People
O _____
O _____
O _____

Follow Up With 5-10 People Potentials, Customers, and Team Members

- O _____
- O _____
- O _____
- O _____
- O _____
- O _____
- O _____
- O _____
- O _____
- O _____

HOT Prospects and Notes:

_____

_____

_____

_____

_____

_____

_____

_____

_____

_____

Personal Development
- O Training Video _____
- O Reading _____

I can do all things through Christ which strengtheneth me.
Phillipians 4:13

Date: _____

O Prayer and Affirmations

Facebook
O Personal Post
O Business Post
O Birthdays
O Add 3 New Friends
    O _____
    O _____
    O _____

Message 5-10 New People Build Relationships & Invite to Learn More
O _____
O _____
O _____
O _____
O _____
O _____
O _____
O _____
O _____
O _____

Present Business or Products to 1-3 People
O _____
O _____
O _____

Follow Up With 5-10 People Potentials, Customers, and Team Members

O _____
O _____
O _____
O _____
O _____
O _____
O _____
O _____
O _____
O _____

HOT Prospects and Notes:

_____
_____
_____
_____
_____
_____
_____
_____
_____
_____
_____

Personal Development
O Training Video _____
O Reading _____

I can do all things through Christ which strengtheneth me.
Phillipians 4:13

Date: _____

O Prayer and Affirmations

Facebook
O Personal Post
O Business Post
O Birthdays
O Add 3 New Friends
    O _____
    O _____
    O _____

Message 5-10 New People   Build Relationships & Invite to Learn More
O _____
O _____
O _____
O _____
O _____
O _____
O _____
O _____
O _____
O _____

Present Business or Products to 1-3 People
O _____
O _____
O _____

Follow Up With 5-10 People Potentials, Customers, and Team Members

O _____

O _____

O _____

O _____

O _____

O _____

O _____

O _____

O _____

O _____

HOT Prospects and Notes:

_____

_____

_____

_____

_____

_____

_____

_____

_____

_____

Personal Development
O Training Video _____

O Reading _____

I can do all things through Christ which strengtheneth me.
Phillipians 4:13

Date: _____

O Prayer and Affirmations

Facebook
O Personal Post
O Business Post
O Birthdays
O Add 3 New Friends
    O _____
    O _____
    O _____

Message 5-10 New People Build Relationships & Invite to Learn More
O _____
O _____
O _____
O _____
O _____
O _____
O _____
O _____
O _____
O _____

Present Business or Products to 1-3 People
O _____
O _____
O _____

Follow Up With 5-10 People _{Potentials, Customers, and Team Members}

O _____
O _____
O _____
O _____
O _____
O _____
O _____
O _____
O _____
O _____

HOT Prospects and Notes:

_____
_____
_____
_____
_____
_____
_____
_____
_____
_____

Personal Development
O Training Video _____
O Reading _____

I can do all things through Christ which strengtheneth me.
Phillipians 4:13

Date: _____

O Prayer and Affirmations

Facebook
O Personal Post
O Business Post
O Birthdays
O Add 3 New Friends
    O _____
    O _____
    O _____

Message 5-10 New People Build Relationships & Invite to Learn More
O _____
O _____
O _____
O _____
O _____
O _____
O _____
O _____
O _____
O _____

Present Business or Products to 1-3 People
O _____
O _____
O _____

Follow Up With 5-10 People Potentials, Customers, and Team Members

O _____

O _____

O _____

O _____

O _____

O _____

O _____

O _____

O _____

O _____

HOT Prospects and Notes:

_____

_____

_____

_____

_____

_____

_____

_____

_____

_____

Personal Development
O Training Video _____

O Reading _____

I can do all things through Christ which strengtheneth me.
Phillipians 4:13

Date: _____

○ Prayer and Affirmations

Facebook
○ Personal Post
○ Business Post
○ Birthdays
○ Add 3 New Friends
    ○ _____
    ○ _____
    ○ _____

Message 5-10 New People Build Relationships & Invite to Learn More
○ _____
○ _____
○ _____
○ _____
○ _____
○ _____
○ _____
○ _____
○ _____
○ _____

Present Business or Products to 1-3 People
○ _____
○ _____
○ _____

Follow Up With 5-10 People Potentials, Customers, and Team Members

O _____
O _____
O _____
O _____
O _____
O _____
O _____
O _____
O _____
O _____

HOT Prospects and Notes:

_____
_____
_____
_____
_____
_____
_____
_____
_____
_____

Personal Development
O Training Video _____
O Reading _____

I can do all things through Christ which strengtheneth me.
Phillipians 4:13

Date: _____

O Prayer and Affirmations

Facebook
O Personal Post
O Business Post
O Birthdays
O Add 3 New Friends
    O _____
    O _____
    O _____

Message 5-10 New People Build Relationships & Invite to Learn More
O _____
O _____
O _____
O _____
O _____
O _____
O _____
O _____
O _____
O _____

Present Business or Products to 1-3 People
O _____
O _____
O _____

Follow Up With 5-10 People Potentials, Customers, and Team Members

O _____
O _____
O _____
O _____
O _____
O _____
O _____
O _____
O _____
O _____

HOT Prospects and Notes:

_____
_____
_____
_____
_____
_____
_____
_____
_____
_____
_____

Personal Development
O Training Video _____
O Reading _____

I can do all things through Christ which strengtheneth me.
Phillipians 4:13

Date: _____

O Prayer and Affirmations

Facebook
O Personal Post
O Business Post
O Birthdays
O Add 3 New Friends
    O _____
    O _____
    O _____

Message 5-10 New People Build Relationships & Invite to Learn More
O _____
O _____
O _____
O _____
O _____
O _____
O _____
O _____
O _____
O _____

Present Business or Products to 1-3 People
O _____
O _____
O _____

Follow Up With 5-10 People Potentials, Customers, and Team Members

○ _____
○ _____
○ _____
○ _____
○ _____
○ _____
○ _____
○ _____
○ _____
○ _____

HOT Prospects and Notes:

_____

_____

_____

_____

_____

_____

_____

_____

_____

Personal Development
○ Training Video _____
○ Reading _____

I can do all things through Christ which strengtheneth me.
Phillipians 4:13

Date: _____

O Prayer and Affirmations

Facebook
O Personal Post
O Business Post
O Birthdays
O Add 3 New Friends
     O _____
     O _____
     O _____

Message 5-10 New People Build Relationships & Invite to Learn More
O _____
O _____
O _____
O _____
O _____
O _____
O _____
O _____
O _____
O _____

Present Business or Products to 1-3 People
O _____
O _____
O _____

Follow Up With 5-10 People Potentials, Customers, and Team Members

O _____
O _____
O _____
O _____
O _____
O _____
O _____
O _____
O _____
O _____

HOT Prospects and Notes:

_____
_____
_____
_____
_____
_____
_____
_____
_____
_____
_____

Personal Development
O Training Video _____
O Reading _____

I can do all things through Christ which strengtheneth me.
Phillipians 4:13

IT'S TIME TO ORDER YOUR NEXT 90 DAY IPA JOURNAL!

Date: _____

O Prayer and Affirmations

Facebook
O Personal Post
O Business Post
O Birthdays
O Add 3 New Friends
    O _____
    O _____
    O _____

Message 5-10 New People Build Relationships & Invite to Learn More
O _____
O _____
O _____
O _____
O _____
O _____
O _____
O _____
O _____
O _____

Present Business or Products to 1-3 People
O _____
O _____
O _____

Follow Up With 5-10 People Potentials, Customers, and Team Members

- ○ _____
- ○ _____
- ○ _____
- ○ _____
- ○ _____
- ○ _____
- ○ _____
- ○ _____
- ○ _____
- ○ _____

HOT Prospects and Notes:

_____

_____

_____

_____

_____

_____

_____

_____

_____

_____

Personal Development
- ○ Training Video _____
- ○ Reading _____

I can do all things through Christ which strengtheneth me.
Phillipians 4:13

Date: _____

O Prayer and Affirmations

Facebook
O Personal Post
O Business Post
O Birthdays
O Add 3 New Friends
      O _____
      O _____
      O _____

Message 5-10 New People Build Relationships & Invite to Learn More
O _____
O _____
O _____
O _____
O _____
O _____
O _____
O _____
O _____
O _____

Present Business or Products to 1-3 People
O _____
O _____
O _____

Follow Up With 5-10 People Potentials, Customers, and Team Members

O _____
O _____
O _____
O _____
O _____
O _____
O _____
O _____
O _____
O _____

HOT Prospects and Notes:

_____
_____
_____
_____
_____
_____
_____
_____
_____
_____

Personal Development
O Training Video _____
O Reading _____

I can do all things through Christ which strengtheneth me.
Phillipians 4:13

Date: _____

O Prayer and Affirmations

Facebook
O Personal Post
O Business Post
O Birthdays
O Add 3 New Friends
    O _____
    O _____
    O _____

Message 5-10 New People   Build Relationships & Invite to Learn More
O _____
O _____
O _____
O _____
O _____
O _____
O _____
O _____
O _____
O _____

Present Business or Products to 1-3 People
O _____
O _____
O _____

Follow Up With 5-10 People Potentials, Customers, and Team Members

O _____
O _____
O _____
O _____
O _____
O _____
O _____
O _____
O _____
O _____

HOT Prospects and Notes:

_____
_____
_____
_____
_____
_____
_____
_____
_____
_____

Personal Development
O Training Video _____
O Reading _____

I can do all things through Christ which strengtheneth me.
Phillipians 4:13

Date: _____

O Prayer and Affirmations

Facebook
O Personal Post
O Business Post
O Birthdays
O Add 3 New Friends
    O _____
    O _____
    O _____

Message 5-10 New People   Build Relationships & Invite to Learn More
O _____
O _____
O _____
O _____
O _____
O _____
O _____
O _____
O _____
O _____

Present Business or Products to 1-3 People
O _____
O _____
O _____

Follow Up With 5-10 People <small>Potentials, Customers, and Team Members</small>

O _____
O _____
O _____
O _____
O _____
O _____
O _____
O _____
O _____
O _____

HOT Prospects and Notes:

_____

_____

_____

_____

_____

_____

_____

_____

_____

_____

Personal Development
O Training Video _____
O Reading _____

I can do all things through Christ which strengtheneth me.
Phillipians 4:13

Date: _____

O Prayer and Affirmations

Facebook
O Personal Post
O Business Post
O Birthdays
O Add 3 New Friends
    O _____
    O _____
    O _____

Message 5-10 New People Build Relationships & Invite to Learn More
O _____
O _____
O _____
O _____
O _____
O _____
O _____
O _____
O _____
O _____

Present Business or Products to 1-3 People
O _____
O _____
O _____

Follow Up With 5-10 People Potentials, Customers, and Team Members

O _____

O _____

O _____

O _____

O _____

O _____

O _____

O _____

O _____

O _____

HOT Prospects and Notes:

_____

_____

_____

_____

_____

_____

_____

_____

_____

Personal Development
O Training Video _____

O Reading _____

I can do all things through Christ which strengtheneth me.
Phillipians 4:13

Date: _____

O Prayer and Affirmations

Facebook
O Personal Post
O Business Post
O Birthdays
O Add 3 New Friends
    O _____
    O _____
    O _____

Message 5-10 New People Build Relationships & Invite to Learn More
O _____
O _____
O _____
O _____
O _____
O _____
O _____
O _____
O _____
O _____

Present Business or Products to 1-3 People
O _____
O _____
O _____

Follow Up With 5-10 People Potentials, Customers, and Team Members

O _____
O _____
O _____
O _____
O _____
O _____
O _____
O _____
O _____
O _____

HOT Prospects and Notes:

_____
_____
_____
_____
_____
_____
_____
_____
_____
_____

Personal Development
O Training Video _____
O Reading _____

I can do all things through Christ which strengtheneth me.
Phillipians 4:13

Date: _____

O Prayer and Affirmations

Facebook
O Personal Post
O Business Post
O Birthdays
O Add 3 New Friends
     O _____
     O _____
     O _____

Message 5-10 New People Build Relationships & Invite to Learn More
O _____
O _____
O _____
O _____
O _____
O _____
O _____
O _____
O _____
O _____

Present Business or Products to 1-3 People
O _____
O _____
O _____

Follow Up With 5-10 People Potentials, Customers, and Team Members

○ _____
○ _____
○ _____
○ _____
○ _____
○ _____
○ _____
○ _____
○ _____
○ _____

HOT Prospects and Notes:

_____
_____
_____
_____
_____
_____
_____
_____
_____
_____

Personal Development
○ Training Video _____
○ Reading _____

I can do all things through Christ which strengtheneth me.
Phillipians 4:13

Date: _____

O Prayer and Affirmations

Facebook
O Personal Post
O Business Post
O Birthdays
O Add 3 New Friends
    O _____
    O _____
    O _____

Message 5-10 New People Build Relationships & Invite to Learn More
O _____
O _____
O _____
O _____
O _____
O _____
O _____
O _____
O _____
O _____

Present Business or Products to 1-3 People
O _____
O _____
O _____

Follow Up With 5-10 People <small>Potentials, Customers, and Team Members</small>

O _____

O _____

O _____

O _____

O _____

O _____

O _____

O _____

O _____

O _____

HOT Prospects and Notes:

_____

_____

_____

_____

_____

_____

_____

_____

_____

_____

Personal Development
O Training Video _____

O Reading _____

I can do all things through Christ which strengtheneth me.
Phillipians 4:13

Date: _____

○ Prayer and Affirmations

Facebook
○ Personal Post
○ Business Post
○ Birthdays
○ Add 3 New Friends
    ○ _____
    ○ _____
    ○ _____

Message 5-10 New People Build Relationships & Invite to Learn More
○ _____
○ _____
○ _____
○ _____
○ _____
○ _____
○ _____
○ _____
○ _____
○ _____

Present Business or Products to 1-3 People
○ _____
○ _____
○ _____

Follow Up With 5-10 People Potentials, Customers, and Team Members

O _____
O _____
O _____
O _____
O _____
O _____
O _____
O _____
O _____
O _____

HOT Prospects and Notes:

_____
_____
_____
_____
_____
_____
_____
_____
_____
_____

Personal Development
O Training Video _____
O Reading _____

I can do all things through Christ which strengtheneth me.
Phillipians 4:13

Date: _____

O Prayer and Affirmations

Facebook
O Personal Post
O Business Post
O Birthdays
O Add 3 New Friends
    O _____
    O _____
    O _____

Message 5-10 New People Build Relationships & Invite to Learn More
O _____
O _____
O _____
O _____
O _____
O _____
O _____
O _____
O _____
O _____

Present Business or Products to 1-3 People
O _____
O _____
O _____

Follow Up With 5-10 People Potentials, Customers, and Team Members

O _____

O _____

O _____

O _____

O _____

O _____

O _____

O _____

O _____

O _____

HOT Prospects and Notes:

_____

_____

_____

_____

_____

_____

_____

_____

_____

_____

Personal Development

O Training Video _____

O Reading _____

I can do all things through Christ which strengtheneth me.
Phillipians 4:13

Made in the USA
Columbia, SC
12 December 2021

51177410R00104